PUB

LANCASHIRE WITCHES TRAIL

Valerie Yewdall

Illustrations by Jane Fielder

ISBN 0 9531256 1 0
First Published 1999
Text - Valerie Yewdall
Illustrations - Jane Fielder

Whilst the author has walked and researched all the routes and sampled the food at all the pubs mentioned, no responsibility can be accepted for any change of circumstances.

Title page illustration - Lancaster Prison (journey's end)

Published by VALDONIA
3 Rushcroft Terrace, Baildon, Shipley, West Yorks BD17 6DA

Printed by:
Carnmor Print & Design, 95-97 London Road, Preston, Lancashire. PR1 4BA

CONTENTS

Miles Page

Acknowledgements

Thanks to Judy, Jane and Eileen for their invaluable help.

A faithful friend is a strong defence;
and he that hath found such a one hath found a treasure.
Ecclesiastes

This is a book for those who enjoy walking combined with a pub lunch. If one starts a walk at a pub, it not only provides a place of refreshment, but also a focal point. Many publicans have no objection to your leaving your car in their car park provided you have participated in their wares and are courteous enough to ask. The walks vary in length to suit all tastes. Some involve climbing to a viewpoint - well worth the effort in my opinion. For all walks, boots, waterproofs and the relevant map are recommended. I have tried to combine visits to interesting pubs, pleasant walks and a glimpse of the past in this book. I hope you will gain as much enjoyment as I did compiling them.
Bon appétit and put your best foot forward!

Previous publications:
Pub Walks in Harrogate & the Wharfe Valley
Pub Walks in Haworth & the Aire Valley
Pub Walks in Ilkley & Wharfedale District
Pub Walks in Otley & the Washburn Valley
Pub Walks in Pendle District

Introduction

This book follows on from my Pendle Pub Walks book. Firstly we climb the notorious Pendle Hill, the scene of much mystery and history. It dominates the countryside and can be seen for miles around. It ascends to just below 2,000ft. The climb is gradual and the top is a vast flat plateau with excellent views on a clear day. If you are lucky you may catch a glimpse of the Irish Sea and Blackpool Tower glistening in the sunlight.

We then gradually make our route to Lancaster following the Witches Trail, calling at all the pubs on the way of course, and not forgetting a walk from each one. This was the route taken by the condemned witches in 1612. Demdike and Chattox, the two most well known, lived under Pendle Hill and one of the walks in my previous book took us past the site of their former dwelling. They, and others, were brought before Justice Roger Nowell and confessed to witchcraft. They were sent to Lancaster Castle to await trial. Demdike died in prison before the trial. The conditions were terrible. The gaoler received no salary and had to extract money from the inmates. Woe betide the prisoners if they had no money to offer for the most rudimentary requirements. Due to the insanitary conditions there was much gaol fever, which killed many more than did the hangman. They were locked up in underground dungeons and almost starved to death on a diet of water-soup, bread boiled in water.

Executions of the condemned took place at Gallows Hill, where stood a permanent gallows. The prisoners were huddled together in the bottom of a springless cart with their coffins piled up behind them. They stopped at the Golden Lion public house where they were allowed a last drink, which was naturally made to last as long as possible. One unlucky person refused a drink on temperance grounds and was hanged. If he had taken a drink his life would have been spared, for his reprieve had arrived at the prison, but too late to stay the execution.

The executions were regarded as a day out and vast mobs congregated to see the end of the unfortunates. On August 20th 1612 nine were hung, convicted of witchcraft, in front of a huge crowd of jeering people. Their bodies were then burnt as they were not allowed to be buried in consecrated ground. The last witch to be burnt alive was in 1613 at Pocklington, North Yorkshire.

We shall never know whether they were truly malevolent people with powers of evil or innocents taking the blame for all unfortunate but natural occurrences.

The Pendle Inn is an imposing stone structure, built in 1930. Inside, it is oak panelled with comfortable red plush carpet and seating with the original open fireplaces. There is a Games Room. En-suite accommodation is available with colour TV, tea and coffee facilities for those walking the Pendle Way, or wishing to explore this delightful area. Lunches and evening meals are provided of home prepared food of ample portions and reasonably priced.

The Inn is situated under the lee of mystical Pendle Hill, which at 1831 feet, dominates the landscape. Here has been the site of much history. At the end of November 1536, there was a rebellion against the suppression of the Catholic religion by Henry VIII. There was loyalty to the king, but a need for freedom of worship. Beacons were erected on Pendle Hill, and their lighting to be taken as a summons to arms.

In 1646, George Fox was said to have climbed Pendle Hill, and had a revelation. Thereafter, he preached a gospel of love and founded the Quakers. He was frequently imprisoned for his beliefs, but won many followers.

- **Start:** The Pendle Inn, Barley. Tel: 01282 614808
- **Distance:** 6 miles
- **Map:** Outdoor Leisure 41. Forest of Bowland. Grid:- 822 404
- **Access:** From Barrowford Bridge turn left on the road to Nelson. Turn first right at the White Bear on Pasture Lane to Roughlee, left to Barley
- **Terrain:** This is the hardest walk in the book, but the most rewarding. The climb is gradual and the descent steep. There is an alternative route to avoid the climb if necessary. Choose a clear day.

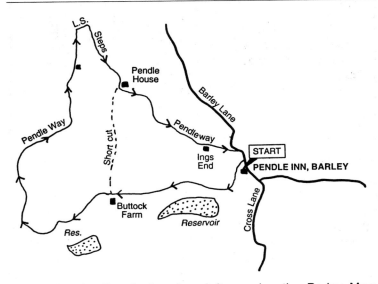

On leaving the Pendle Inn, turn left, passing the Barley Mow Restaurant.

Opposite the Tea Rooms, turn left over a hidden stile into a field. Round the side of a bungalow to a gate. Bear left to a stile in the corner. Continue to bear left on to a ladder stile. Ahead on a grass track to a stile and gate, ahead to gate. Follow the line of trees on the left to follow a good track to Ogden Hill. Ever upwards with the

7

ditch on the right to a wall at Buttock Farm. (This is where you could turn right following the wall to avoid the climb.) Follow the wall on the left to reach Upper Ogden Reservoir, dropping down to Deep Clough Spring and joining the Pendle Way turning right and following the clear marked path leading to the summit at the trig. point at Beacon or Big End. This is a great vantage point looking to the North West across the Forest of Bowland, the distant Lakeland Fells, Ribblesdale and the Three Peaks, Craven Fells, and if you are very lucky you may even see the sun on the Irish Sea and Blackpool Tower.

Continue on the ridge to a ladder stile. Turn right, following the wall to a stile in it and a Pendle Way stone post. Follow down the steep steps to reach Pendle House and the wall, if you had taken the easy route. Bear right to the back of the house to a gate. Down the field to a gate, ahead to a stile to reach Ing Ends Farm. Follow the wall on the left and the beck on the right on the Pendle Way to enter an enclosed way to reach a lane. Turn left, then right over a bridge, following the beck on the left to reach the road.

Turn right back to the Pendle Inn.

Summit of Pendle Hill

Ye Old Sparrowhawk is to be found in the quiet village of Fence, thus named as at one time there was a store of deer here, kept safe behind a fence.

It is here also that Robert Nutter of Greenhead died, reputedly as a result of witchcraft by Ann Whittle, alias Chattox for which she was hung at Lancaster Castle.

There has been a building on the site of the Sparrowhawk since the 17th century. The original building was a farmhouse and was sold in 1812 to Robert Hargreaves, known as the Sparrow Hawk, when it became a public house.

Today the Inn will certainly bewitch you with its delightful setting, flagged floors, old beams and open log fires. There is much of interest to see including old photos, stained-glass windows, 32 species of British birds, witty sayings and the writings on the wall.

The Inn is open for morning coffee, lunch, afternoon tea and evening meals. The food is excellent, tasty, reasonably priced and with ample portions. I highly recommend this establishment.

- **Start:** Ye Old Sparrowhawk, Wheatley Lane, Fence. Tel: ~~01282 614126~~ 01282 603034
- **Distance:** 4 miles
- **Map:** Outdoor Leisure 41, Forest of Bowland & Ribblesdale. Grid Ref: 840 385
- **Access:** From Barrowford Bridge turn second right to Wheatley Lane, off A682 to Nelson road
- **Terrain:** A pleasant walk with excellent views. Some upward sections. Much of interest in Newchurch.

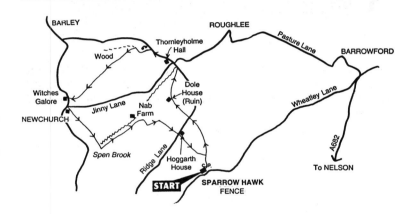

From the right-hand corner of the Sparrowhawk car park follow the Witches Trail at the side of a beck. Climb up the field to reach a stile in a stone wall. Quickly cross to the other side of the wall. Now the stream is on the left. Head forwards and follow the wall on the left to reach the road.

Straight across following the wall on the left. At the end of the wall continue straight forward following the large stones on the left to a gate at a derelict building. Diagonally right to a stile in a wire fence, then diagonally left to a gate in the corner leading to the road.

Turn left and on the road to Barley, passing Thorneyholme Hall. Up the hill, before the telephone box turn left on a lane leading to a farm, climbing upwards. Turn left at the Witches sign, following the

Thorneyholme Hall

wall on the left to cross a stile, wall and wood on the right. (Now on the ridge with excellent vista, Pendle Hill to the right.) Enter the wood ahead. Bear left to a stile at the end of the wood, bear right to the road at Newchurch.

Turn left passing Witches Galore shop.

Witches Galore Shop

The Witches Galore shop is known all over the world. The present owner has been here for 16 years and has built up a vast trade in everything connected with the Witches of Pendle. Be sure to investigate further and do not miss the poster with the word for witch in 42 languages!

Turn left to enter St. Mary's church. After inspection proceed in front of the church to the metal gate. Turn right with the wall on the right down the field to reach the road at Spenbrook.

St. Mary's, Newchurch

There was a Chapel of Ease on this site in 1250, but the first stone church was built in 1544, known as the New Church. The tower is the only part remaining of the original structure. Here can be found the famous 'Eye of God', constructed in stone with a slate in-fill to represent the pupil. This was supposed to protect people from evil. It did not prevent the witch Chattox from exhuming 3 skulls and removing their teeth for use in her spells. Reputedly, near the church porch is the grave of another witch, Alice Nutter, though this is unlikely to be true as condemned witches were never buried in consecrated ground.

Turn left passing the sewage works on a clear lane with the brook on the left. At Lower Dimperley Farm and a road junction turn right leading up to Higher Graystones and a Witches sign. Follow the drive to the road.

Straight across and down the right-hand side of Hoggarth House. Follow the fence on the right to go through two gates at the bottom. Diagonally left across the field to a gate in the corner. Turn right, over stile, diagonally across the field on the outward track to return to the Sparrowhawk.

The Assheton Arms
Downham

The Assheton Arms takes its name from the Lordship of the Manor of Downham which has been held by the Assheton family for over 400 years. Richard Assheton purchased the Manor House in 1558. He is alleged to have been "bewitched to death" by Anne Whittle, better known as Mother Chattox.

Downham is both unique and picturesque. It is still owned by the Asshetons who maintain its traditions and authenticity. There is no electric street lighting or yellow lines and for his reason many films have been made here - Whistle Down the Wind with Hayley Mills and A Likely Lad.

Over the door to the Inn you will find the coat-of-arms of the Asshetons Nec Arrogo, Nec Dubito - neither arrogance nor doubt. This will certainly be found in the friendly atmosphere and there is no doubt you will leave suitably refreshed after your traditional or continental fare. Lunches and evening meals are served in this cosy corner with its open, original fireplace dated 1765 and its pew seats.

Look for the wooden busts of guardsmen wearing busby hats; in fact newel posts from the Busby department store once on Manningham Lane, Bradford. Members of the Busby family manage the Assheton Arms.

- **Start:** The Assheton Arms, Downham. Tel: 01200 441227
- **Distance:** 5¹/₂ miles
- **Map:** Outdoor Leisure 41. Grid Ref: 785 444
- **Access:** From Barrowford Bridge turn up the side of the White Bear in Barley Lane, left on Pendle Road to Downham
- **Terrain:** Pleasant riverside paths and rolling countryside. Open, spectacular views.

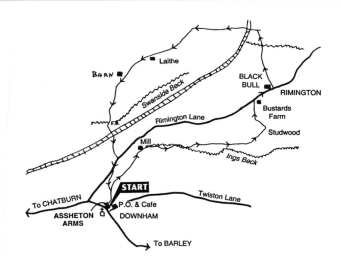

From the car park behind the Assheton Arms turn immediately left past the bungalow. Follow the wall on the left (Pendle Hill behind you). At a marked post turn diagonally right, down the field and heading right between the hillocks down to a stile in the corner by the Old Mill. Across to a sign and stile, turning right leading to a clear track. Follow the beck on the left to cross at a bridge. Continue with the beck on the right. Cross a stile and later cross again at a wooden plank bridge. Head up the field towards Stub Wood Farm, up to a marked tree by a gate. Follow the signs to Rimmington leading to a lane. Turn left, up the drive to the road.

Turn right to the Black Bull (an alternative start to the walk).

14

The Black Bull
Rimington

This a unique country inn, owned by Michael and Barbara who personally supervise the running of this remarkable place. They had emigrated to Canada, but found that they still pined for a view of Pendle, so in 1993 they returned to purchase the present building which had been empty for some time. They brought with them a collection of signed pictures of the wildlife of Canada, which can be seen displayed in the cosy, intimate dining room.

They also brought with them a great enthusiasm for steam engines and old railway memorabilia. They lovingly and painstakingly restored the building to its present first class state. The walls display photos, name and number plates of famous engines: Canadian Pacific, Royal Scot and Great Western line. There is a large model engine in a glass case, and train departure times from Blackpool.

The whole place is a wealth of interest, especially to the railway enthusiast.

The service and food is first class with a most succulent menu. This is a most interesting and popular place, be sure to visit this one.

Turn down the right side of the Black Bull, across a track and down the field and over a bridge and stile. Turn left and left over a bridge. Under the railway tunnel. Follow the fence on the right to a gate. Turn left on an enclosed way to a stile on the right. Head up the hill to a gate ahead. Bear left to pass a pond/tip on the right to a stile by a gate. Head for the wood and gate (Pendle Hill on the left). Follow the fence on the right heading for Swanside Laithe. Continue to follow the fence on the right for nearly ½ mile to a barn. Bear left to a gate, follow the fence on the right down to a gate. Down to an old packhorse bridge. Turn left briefly to a stile. Follow the fence on the left, under a tunnel, leading to the road.

Turn right passing a barn. Turn left at the footpath sign. Bear right up the field, following the wall on the right leading back to the car park at the Assheton Arms. Before leaving investigate the church and the post office which is also a café.

Downham Post Office & Tea Rooms

Providing light lunches and afternoon teas of homemade cakes with a witches flavour. It is a cosy and intimate setting to relax after your walk. Bed and breakfast accommodation is also available.
The shop is well stocked with local books, witches in all shapes and sizes and many more souvenirs.

St. Leonard's Church, Downham

St. Leonard's Church, Downham has Saxon or early Norman foundations. The list of clergy dates back to 1541. St. Leonard is the patron saint of country folk. The present parish includes Downham and Twiston. It was once of Chapel of Whalley in the days of the abbey. The living is now in the hands of the Rt. Hon. Lord Clitheroe who lives in Downham Hall. There is a private entrance gate from the Hall to the churchyard. The beautiful stained-glass window was constructed by Ralph and Richard Assheton in 1869.

The Asshetons took possession of the Hall in 1558, it was centuries old then and belonged to the Dinelays. Downham comes from Dunum, meaning "many hills". As you look around you will see them.

The architecture is varied, Tudor buildings near the bridge, 18th-century handloom, weavers' cottages round the green and the Georgian Hall set in its own private enclosed gardens near the church. There is evidence of Roman occupation by a large stone by the Hall entrance which is thought to mark the grave of two legionnaires

The outside of the Brown Cow at Chatburn is painted an attractive black and white and on my visit was decorated with hanging baskets of pansies.

You will find a warm welcome inside with food of ample portions and reasonable prices. There is an intimate restaurant in addition to bar snacks.

The beams of the Inn are decorated with a display of horse brasses and jugs. There are old prints of the area on the walls. The bench seating all round is comfortable and there is a secluded beer garden to the rear.

The Inn lies on a former Roman road between Ribchester and Ilkley, built 2000 years ago

- **Start:** The Brown Cow, Chatburn. Tel: 01200 441272
- **Distance:** 7$\frac{1}{2}$ miles
- **Map:** Outdoor Leisure 41. Grid Ref: 768 442
- **Access:** Off the A59 Gisburn to Clitheroe Road
- **Terrain:** Partly on the Ribble Way. Very pleasant riverside path. Great variety. Some roadwork. Plenty of refreshment stops. Choose a dry spell.

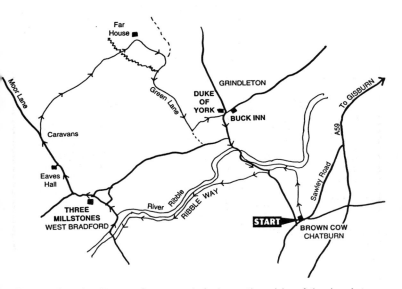

On leaving the Brown Cow turn left down the side of the Inn into a field. Follow the fence on the right, bearing right, passing a sewage works, to reach the River Ribble.

Turn left to follow the river to the road. Turn left to the signpost on the right to West Bradford. Follow the Ribble Way turning right and entering a wood. Drop down to the riverbank and follow it to the bridge. Turn right over it following the road into West Bradford; a charming village with a stream running through and access to the houses by means of quaint old bridges.

Continue up the road to reach the main road. Turn left to the Three Millstones.

After refreshment continue up the road to the signpost on the right. Continue on the enclose way passing a tiny graveyard and up to the road.

Turn right passing Eaves Hall on the left and the Three Rivers Country Caravan Park. Turn right up the steps at the sign. Follow the wire fence on the left to a gate on the left. Forward on a track to the top right-hand corner. Follow the dog-exercise area round to the riding stables and a lane.

Three Millstones
West Bradford

This is a building of great antiquity, being over 400 years old and a former coaching inn. It has a resident ghost, a former highway man called Kirkam Jack who used to frequent the Inn.

There is much character here with its sparkling copper-topped tables and brassware, beamed ceiling, open fires and pew-type seating.

There is a spacious restaurant specialising in fresh fish dishes or bar meals, at lunch times and evenings. I had a delicious homemade leek and potato soups with a most satisfying chunk of granary bread.

The food is attractively served and the portions generous. Theakstons beer.

Walk continued -

Turn right to a gate past a black and white house (Drake House), entering a wood. Cross the beck, turn right following the track to a gate ahead. Immediately right to a stile. Follow the fence on the left to exit onto a road.

Turn left to a junction. Bear right to Lawcock's Farm. Through the farmyard to a gate and stile ahead leading to the left of Lawcock Waterworks. Follow the fence on the right down to a bridge over West Clough Brook. Up to a gate, ahead, fence on the left to reach

The Duke of York was sold at the Swan in Clitheroe in 1832 when it included stables, a brewhouse, pig cote and hen house.

There have been many Dukes of York since the title was created by Richard II. The claim to the throne of Richard, Duke of York led to the Wars of the Roses between Lancashire and Yorkshire. At the battle of Wakefield in 1460 the Yorkists were defeated and Richard slain. A year later the Lancastrians were defeated and Edward IV came to the throne.

Today there seems no animosity towards a Yorkshire lass at the Duke of York which has a friendly, cosy atmosphere. There is a restaurant serving rather special food for lunch or dinner.

Walk continued -

the access drive to Far House. Turn right down it to reach Green Lane. Turn right following the track to reach Green Banks House.

Here leave the track, turning left into a field. Follow the wall on the right crossing a stile ahead. Immediately right to a stile. Follow the fence on the left, down to a bridge over Grindleton Brook and up to the road to reach the Duke of York and The Buck Inn.

The Buck Inn
Grindleton

The Buck Inn has a homely atmosphere with a ramblers' room should your boots be dirty. The Inn dates back to the 18th century and was formerly the house of a head groomsman to the local manor. It was licensed in 1870.

On the low beams is a good collection of toby jugs.
Food and refreshments available for the needy.

Walk continued -

If no refreshments are required turn right down the road. At the bottom turn left on the road to Chatburn. Over the bridge and along the road to the footpath sign on the left, leading to the riverside and following the outward track to return to the Brown Cow.

Grindleton

Here in Grindleton there are many weavers' cottages dating from the days when cloth was produced on handlooms and transported by packhorse routes to market. The coming of machinery put an end to individual work by the creation of mills and factories turning out mass-produced goods. The private manufacture of goods in the home was known as the "domestic system". The Industrial Revolution resulted in terrible working conditions for the poor - man, woman and child alike suffered anguish so as to make the mill owners rich.

The Spread Eagle Hotel
Sawley

The Spread Eagle, with its wings spread out, was established as a national emblem by the Romans.

This delightful Inn is approximately 400 years old, note the vast, thick beams. The character remains but the accommodation is luxurious including en-suite bedrooms. Its outstanding restaurant with panoramic views of the Ribble making it an ideal venue for wedding receptions, conferences, etc. The bar is snug and attractive with a warm atmosphere. In the wine cellar the arch roof is similar in design to the 15th century Cistercian abbey, the ruins of which are just across the road.

It was known far and wide 50 years ago as the Inn which served "some grand ham and egg teas". Now it has an Egon Ronay award for excellent food for morning coffee, lunches, including bar snacks and dinners of top class cuisine in the riverside restaurant. Highly recommended.

- **Start:** The Spread Eagle, Sawley. Tel: 01200 441202/441406
- **Distance:** 7 miles
- **Map:** Outdoor Leisure 41. Grid Ref: 775 466
- **Access:** Off the A59 between Clitheroe and Gisburn
- **Terrain:** Great variety, fields, woods, riverside, much of interest en route. Partly on the Ribble Way.

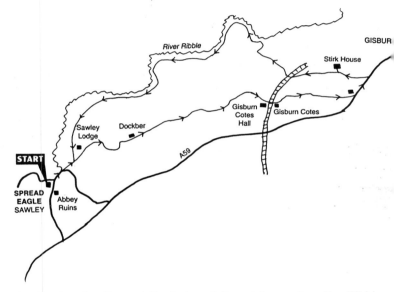

On leaving the Spread Eagle turn left and forward on the Ribble Way. Straight ahead at the entrance to Sawley Lodge, on an enclosed way. Take the gate on the right leaving the main track, leading up to another gate. Turn left on this tarmac track. Over a cattle-grid and up to West Dockber Farm, through the farmyard to the gate ahead. Continue on a clear track to enter an enclosed way (Pendle Hill on the right). Through a gate and **immediately** take the gate on the right. Follow the hedge on the left, turning right at the wood to a stile on the left into a wood. Keep near the fence on the right leading to a stile into a field. Turn left to a stile. Follow the fence on the right to a gate on the right. Diagonally left to a gate. Follow the wire fence on the right to reach Huggan Ing Farm. Turn left off the drive at a stile into a field. Follow the line of trees on the left to a stile. Bear right to Gisburn Cotes Hall, over the railway bridge.

Turn left at the junction to reach Gisburn Cotes Farm. In front of the house to a gate on the right, bear left to the next gate. Diagonally left to a stile. Bear right across the field to a gate. Leading to Leewarden Farm and the main road.

Turn left down the A59 to the entrance to Stirk House. Follow the drive and just before the entrance to the hotel turn left over a stile into a field. Follow the fence on the left to cross over the railway bridge. Follow the fence on the left to a farm gate, leading to a signpost. Follow the route to Fooden Ford. Straight ahead over a stile, fence on the left, turning right down steps and into Steep Wood (a mass of flowering garlic and bluebells on my visit). This track drops down to the River Ribble.

Turn left following it and the Ribble Way direction right back to Sawley Lodge and the outward track. Be sure to see the ruins of Sawley Abbey just beyond the Spread Eagle.

Above all do not lose your desire to walk. Everyday I walk myself into a state of well being and walk away from every illness. I have walked myself into my best thoughts and know of no thought so burdensome that one cannot walk away from it.

Buddha

Stirk House

Stirk House is a most delightful 16th-century manor house and was originally home of the Lister family. Thomas Lister was MP for Clitheroe and died in 1745. Two succeeding Listers became MPs for Clitheroe, one becoming High Sheriff of York and was created Baron Ribblesdale of Gisburn Park in 1797, having raised the 'Yorkshire West Riding Cavalry' that fought in the Napoleonic Wars.

The Hartly family later occupied Stirk House for 150 years.

Mr Adam Tebay lived here from 1868 to 1911 and his granddaughter held her 80th birthday party at the hotel.

The building became licensed in 1935. In 1940 there was a disastrous fire causing the entire roof to collapse. After this the hotel changed hands several times. The present residential proprietors have made extensive improvements - en-suite accommodation, heated swimming pool, sauna, solarium, fitness room and squash courts - all without spoiling the dignified quality of this historical building.

Much of the stonework from the disused Sawley Abbey was used for its construction. There is a Priest Hole in the vast chimney and it is reputed that the face of a monk can be seen peering through the mullioned windows.

Be sure to stop here to appreciate and investigate this lovely house. Of course it could be an alternative start to the walk.

Sawley Abbey

Sawley was once Salley, which means a damp spot where the willow trees grow.

The ruins of Sawley Abbey are all that remains of a once fine Cistercian abbey which was founded in 1147 by Abbot Benedict, twelve brethren and ten converts. William de Percy had been given vast tracts of land by William the Conqueror and was willing to make a gift of land for the abbey in this sheltered valley.

For year the monks laboured to build the abbey and cultivate the land. The site was damp and the winters were bitterly cold. Conditions were hard and the monks wanted to return to Fountains but they were persuaded to stay. They were here for four centuries. The last abbot, Trafford took part in the Pilgrimage of Grace against Henry VIII and for this was hanged. Henry assumed the title of "Defender of the Faith" by Act of Parliament, thus the Church became subordinate to the State. At this time there were more than 600 monastic houses, many extremely wealthy. King Henry coveted this wealth and this led to the Dissolution of the Monasteries in 1537. His reign brought forth religious reforms which altered the whole aspect of English life for ever.

The remains of the abbey are maintained by English Heritage and are open to the public each day.

The Calf's Head Inn
Worston

The Calf's Head is a very superior country inn situated in a delightful setting, nestling at the foot of Pendle Hill in the charming village of Worston.

The building was a former farm and is 250 years old. Today it is most elegant with its oak panelling, comfortable seating and interesting antiques. There is much to see including old prints, Singer sewing machine, Oliver typewriter, bishop's chair and a collection of hub caps from horse-drawn carriages. There is a most beautiful, spacious garden with a stream at the bottom which makes it an ideal setting for wedding receptions.

There are bar meals and an à la carte restaurant offering superb food. En-suite accommodation is also available.

A most surprising place in this quiet backwater.

- **Start:** The Calf's Head, Worston. Tel: 01200 441218
- **Distance:** 6 miles
- **Map:** Outdoor Leisure 41. Grid Ref: 768 427
- **Access:** Off the A59 Gisburn to Clitheroe Road. Turn left after passing under a road bridge
- **Terrain:** Very easy, flat walk, mostly on clear tracks. A refreshment stop halfway round.

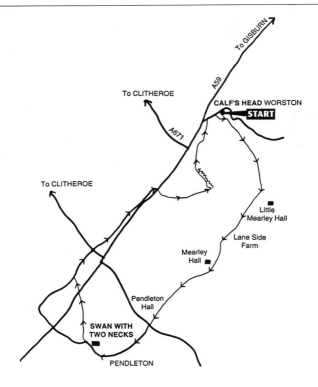

Turn right on leaving The Calf's Head (note the tiny cottage on the left which is reputedly the former dwelling of the convicted witch, Chattox).

Turn right at the footpath sign, round the side of the house to a gate and stile into a field. Follow the wall on the left (Pendle Hill ahead). At the end of the wall, straight ahead to a stile by a tree stump. Ahead up the field, to a small iron gate over a stream. Follow the fence on the right to reach a main track.

Turn right passing Little Mearley Hall on the left. (This was the home of Christopher Nowel. The stonework from the dismantled Sawley Abbey was partly used in its construction. The Hall contains a bay window which was once part of the abbot's dwelling. It is reputed to be haunted by his ghost.)

Over Mearley Brook Bridge. Continue ahead on this clear track to reach Lane Side Farm. Ahead through a gate on the lane to reach Mearley Hall and cottages. Bear right passing Pendleton Hall, over the bridge to the road.

Ahead to Pendleton passing All Saints Church and the National School 1937, to reach The Swan with Two Necks.

After refreshment continue past the Swan with Two Necks, turn right before crossing the bridge to a stile and gate. Bear right with the stream on the left, heading for the road. Over stile and slab by a telegraph pole. Diagonally left to a bridge into a field. Bear left to a stile, at main road. Turn right to a gate on the right, here turn up to the road.

Straight across with care to a stile. Bear right to a bridge, bear left to a gate on to the road.

Turn right to reach the crossroads. Straight ahead on the 'no through road'. At the end it turns up to the main road. Straight across with care. Ahead to the sign, bear left to the gate in the corner, ahead to a small gate, crossing a track. Ahead to reach an attractive bridge, turn left **without crossing it**, stream on the right, to a stile in the corner. Forward to a hidden bridge. Bear right to broken stile, ahead to a stile, diagonally left to a gate onto a lane.

Turn right to the footpath sign on the right, following the stream on the left to the road. Turn left back to The Calf's Head.

The Swan with Two Necks
Pendleton

The origin of this very unusual name is interesting. It is believed that it was in the beginning 'nicks' not necks, referring to the nicks made on the beaks of the birds to mark ownership. Swans were originally only owned by royalty. Elizabeth I granted the privilege of ownership to the Worshipful Company of Vintners and were identified by two nicks on the upper beak. Neck is an obsolete variant of 'nick'. From a sign painters point of view, it would have been easier and more eye catching to depict a swan with two necks.

There are many ornaments of swans with two necks in this cosy village inn. It overlooks the stream which runs through the beautiful village. Bar snacks are served lunch and evening, not to mention the refreshing pint.

Attractively served food at reasonable prices served indoors or outdoors overlooking the stream which flows through the village.

WALK 7:
Dog and Partridge
Barrow

The Dog and Partridge is the local village eatery, dating back to the 18th century when it was built next door to a print works.

There is a cosy, friendly atmosphere here with its intimate restaurant and comfortable bar with pool room. There is an extensive menu offering mouth-watering dishes, served lunch and dinner. The portions are most generous and the prices reasonable.

- **Start:** The Dog & Partridge, Barrow. Tel: 01200 422465
- **Distance:** 6 miles
- **Map:** Outdoor Leisure 41. Grid Ref: 737 384
- **Access:** Turn off the A59 at the roundabout to Clitheroe onto the A671. Turn first left to Barrow
- **Terrain:** An easy, flat walk partly on the Ribble Way and on a Roman road. Much variety and interest en route. Choose a dry spell.

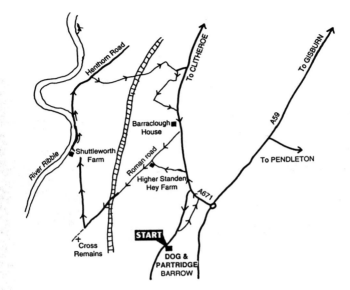

On leaving the Dog and Partridge turn right. After the school, turn right, passing Audley House to reach Thornyholme. Ahead on the grass to a stile in the corner. Follow the hedge on the left to reach the embankment up to the main road.

Turn left and on Clitheroe Road to the footpath sign on the left. Ahead across the field leading to a stile, hedge on the right, leading to a road.

Turn left on this Roman road. Ahead at Higher Standen Hey Farm (noting the very ancient former granary linked to Clitheroe Castle in Roman times).

Through the farmyard, following the arrows and round the side of the farm buildings, turning left through a gate on an enclosed way. Cross the railway line with care. Follow the fence on the right to a stile at a gate, continuing to follow the fence on the right which turns right (before reaching a former cross), to a stile in the corner. Follow the hedge on the right to reach a track leading to Shuttleworth Farm. To the right of the farm (not new house) leading to the Ribble Way. Turn right on Henthorn Road past the waste depot and Mill House. Over a bridge, turn right at the stile. Follow the stream on the right

Ancient granary, now a protected building

All the corn from the area was ground here and the miller took a share which must have been enough to enable him to pay the high rent paid to the Lord of Clitheroe Castle.

and under the railway bridge, ahead to a gate. On an enclosed way to the road.

Turn right and after passing Shireburn Carpets turn right over the bridge to Pendle Cottage. Ahead through the farm onto an enclosed track to a gate ahead. Follow the hedge on the right to a gate. Turn left to the main road.

Turn right and after Barraclough House turn right passing the delightful residence of Long Acre. Turn left at the gate, before the bungalow (on the outward track), follow the hedge on the left to the stile in the corner. Ahead to the road.

Turn right down the road to return to the Dog and Partridge.

The New Inn is far from new. It was formerly a coaching inn named the Market Hotel. The stables are 250 years old and are soon to be converted into a dining area. Be sure to view the garden in the courtyard at the rear. It is most attractive with its artificial grass. Inside there are small cosy rooms with original fireplaces. It has an old world atmosphere with its prints of bygone Clitheroe. It is situated opposite the castle and one can imagine the garrison dropping in here for a pint.

The landlord is genial and happy to supply real ales with a joke or two for good measure.

- ● **Start:** The New Inn, Clitheroe. Tel: 01200 423312
- ● **Distance:** 3¹/2 miles
- ● **Map:** Outdoor Leisure 41. Grid Ref: 741 418
- ● **Access:** Off the A59 on A671 to Clitheroe opposite the castle
- ● **Terrain:** Very easy short walk with time to see castle and museum.

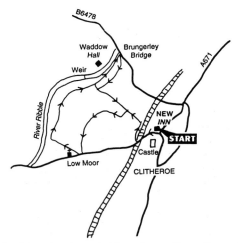

On leaving the New Inn turn right and over the railway bridge. Turn right on Castle View Road. At the end turn left on Kirkmoor Road. At the end turn left on Back Commons Lane. Turn right at the footpath sign by a gate into a field. Forward to a stile, bear right to a kissing gate. Turn left following the fence on the left to a stile in the corner. Bear right to the next marked stile and stile in the corner to enter a narrow enclosed way leading into a field. Follow the trees on the right to enter another enclosed way leading to the road at Low Moor.

Turn right and down St. Paul Street. At the bottom turn right to follow the Ribble Way sign passing the former Wesleyan school dated 1866. Continue on the dirt track passing allotments to reach the river and a weir. (Option here of turning right for a quick return.) On the opposite side of the river is the imposing Waddow Hall, formerly owned by the Garnett family, now a guide training centre.

Continue on the riverside path to reach Brungerley Bridge. Do **not** cross it but turn right in front of the cottage and follow the hedge on the left to a marked stile. Follow the hedge on the left to reach Woodland Burial Grounds. Follow the footpath, with the wood on the right high above the river. When the weir is reached turn left to a gate. Follow the trees on the left to a gate. Ahead to a stile to reach Back Commons Lane. Turn left following the outward route to return to view the castle.

Brungerley Bridge

Brungerley Bridge was built in 1820. Previously there had been stepping-stones to cross the river. This area became industrialised with a mill and weir built to hold the water for power. This resulted in the rising of the river and the need for a bridge. The stepping-stones were a danger especially after a long visit to the pub!

In the late 1800s the river was frozen hard and it was enjoyed by skaters. In summer there was boating and refreshments. Crowds of up to 3,000 came from the Lancashire towns for a day of relaxation and enjoyment from the cotton mills. There were queues of an hour for the boats. On Sunday afternoons Clitheroe Band played, but there were objections to Sunday bathing. Changing huts were provided to satisfy modesty and a notice 'All persons bathing without bathing drawers will be prosecuted!'.

Peg o'Nell was a legendary figure who was reputed to claim a victim at the river crossing every 7 years before the bridge was built.

In 1783 George Battersby forded the river to sell his cattle at Clitheroe Fair. On his return journey he was murdered and his body thrown in the river. On each year on 29th March, the anniversary of his death, the water runs red, so I was told. The four accused of his murder were tried at Lancaster and surprisingly acquitted, so perhaps George was one of Peg O'Nell's victims.

Clitheroe Castle

Clitheroe

Clitheroe is a busy market town, known as the capital of the Ribble Valley. It is dominated by its Norman castle set on a limestone crag, high above the little town. It is 800 years old but when you stand inside the keep, hidden voices tell you of its history. It is reputed to be one of the oldest stone structures dating back to the 12th century.

It was founded by Roger de Poitou, a Norman baron. The site being ideal for defence and to control the vast area bestowed on him by William the Conqueror.

The keep, with its 9 feet thick walls, is all that remains of this one-time gaol and fortress.

In 1919, the owners, Lord Montague of Beaulieu, sold the castle to the people of Clitheroe and it was converted into a memorial to the 260 who lost their lives from Clitheroe.

In 1981 a museum was opened in the castle house telling the history and geology of the area. A most interesting place to visit.

The castle is set in lovely gardens and is open from Easter to the end of October.

WALK 9:
Wellsprings
Pendle Moor

B's Bar Café at the Wellsprings is quite a remarkable place. The outside appearance of this former licensed fish and chip shop is most deceiving. Inside the transformation is quite amazing. Everything is of top quality, from its maple wood floor, chandeliers, exotic plants and fresh flowers on all tables to its superlative views looking to the coast and a glimpse of Blackpool Tower on a clear day. I was most impressed with the friendliness, standard of presentation and quality and variety of dishes on offer. This place has been lovingly converted and is of great pride to the owners. It is next door to a dry ski slope and the roof garden overlooks the slope and glorious Lancashire scenery.

Their motto is "high quality cuisine and service at a price to suit everyone" and that is just what you get.

- ● **Start:** Wellsprings, Pendle Moor. Tel: 01200 427722
- ● **Distance:** 6 miles
- ● **Map:** Outdoor Leisure 41. Grid Ref: 772 390
- ● **Access:** Off the A59 between Worston and Pendleton
- ● **Terrain:** A moorland trod. Can be boggy in places. Choose a clear day. Glorious views.

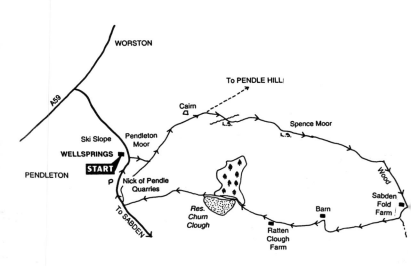

Take the footpath opposite the Inn and ski slope. Up the track, bearing right to reach a clear track.

Turn left up Badger Wells Hill for approximately half a mile. Soon after the cairn, turn right on a green track, leading to a ladder stile. Turn left, following the wall on the left to a ladder stile. Over the wall, turn right on the broad, green track over Spence Moor to a ladder stile. Bear left downwards on a boggy section to a gate. Follow the wall on the right to a gate. Follow the fence round a wood on the right, and down to a farm track leading to Sabden Fold (look out for peacocks here).

At the road turn right along the lane, bear right at the junction. Continue on this good track, turning up to a barn. Turn left on a good track to reach Ratten Clough Farm. Follow the wall on the left to a stile and higher up to reach a gate. Drop down to Churn Clough Reservoir. Turn right, round the reservoir to its head and a gate, and a stile ahead. Follow the wall on the right to reach a clear track, leading to the road.

For a quick return, turn right and follow the road back to Wellsprings. Alternatively, turn right leading to the quarries and a track leading to the outward track, turning left off it to retrace route back to the Inn

Wellsprings

Owd Ned's Tavern and the Stone House Restaurant. This imposing building was formerly Little Mitton Hall and dates back to 1514 when it was built for a cousin of Henry VII. It is one of the finest examples of a manor house, complete with minstrals' gallery, superb woodwork, massive fireplace and stained-glass windows. This is now the stunning dining room where one can banquet in regal splendour. Accommodation is also available at reasonable prices for a longer stay to discover more of this beautiful area and its 18 acres of grounds.

Adjoining is Owd Ned's Tavern with its stone flagged floor and dark oak beams opening onto the light conservatory. It is open from 7am-11pm every day for homemade country fayre to suit all palates and tastes. Children are well catered for. There is a good selection of traditional cask ales, guest beers and lagers to choose from.

Try Ned's Special - prime rump steak, served with a generous portion of mushrooms and onions. All served on a fresh, white baton, topped with cheese. This will last you until your return for afternoon tea!

- **Start:** Mitton Hall or The Aspinall Arms, Little Mitton. Tel: 01254 826544
- **Distance:** 7 miles
- **Map:** Outdoor Leisure 41. Grid Ref: 718 385
- **Access:** Off the A59 on B6246 to Whalley
- **Terrain:** Partly on the Ribble Way. Over fields and some roadwork. Many refreshment stops on route. Much of interest to see.

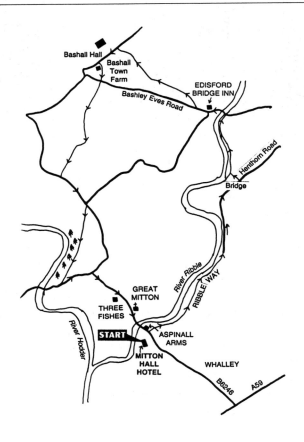

The Aspinall Arms
Little Mitton

The Aspinall Arms is an interesting hostelry, named after a local family who lived in Little Mitton Hall. Here is the site of the former boat house for the ferry which crossed the Ribble to Great Mitton. The river formed the boundary between Lancashire and Yorkshire. In 1974 the boundaries were altered and both Little and Great Mitton were encompassed in Lancashire.

The inn provides good food in relaxed setting either indoors or in the riverside gardens. Note the coat-of-arms, Accis, Fortissima & Virtus - Duty, Fortitude & Virtue.

On leaving Mitton Hall turn left to the Aspinall Arms. Turn right in front of it to reach the Ribble. Follow the river for 1½ miles to reach a bridge. Over it turn left, first right and immediately left into a field to reach the river. Follow it to Edisford Bridge. Cross the bridge to reach Edisford Bridge Inn (time for refreshment?).

Turn right on Bashall Eaves Road to the signpost on the right. Diagonally across the field to a stile in the corner. Follow the fence on the left to reach a drive and a stile opposite. Ahead to a stile in a hedge, turn right to a gate, through a gap, ahead to a gate, to the road.

Turn left (Bashall Hall on the right). Ahead to turn left in front of Bashall Town Farm on a quiet lane to cross a road to a gate opposite and one ahead, to reach a gate in the left-hand corner. Continue in the same direction through gates to reach an enclosed track. Follow it to a marked gate towards a mill conversion to reach a road. Pass Withgill Lodge to reach the main road.

Turn left to reach a junction. Turn right on the B6243 to Hirst Green to the signpost to Hodder Bridge. Bear right across the large field to reach a stile into a wood. Soon exit the wood and follow the fence on the right to reach the road.

Turn left and right at a junction to reach the Three Fishes and a little further All Hollows Church, the Aspinall Arms and Mitton Hall.

Mitton Hall Hotel

Edisford Bridge Inn
Clitheroe

Edisford Bridge Inn was the site of a battle in 1138. King David of Scotland invaded England and there was a battle with the Normans. The Scots were victorious and the river was said to have run red with Norman blood.

There was also a leper hospital here in Norman times. The disease was widespread in those days when fresh fruit and vegetables were a rarity. Nothing remains of the hospital today, but it is likely to have been the first built in the country.

The present Inn adjoins a working farm and is a very popular venue with a warm welcome. There is an extensive menu, including a children's menu and a fine wine list. All the food is appetising and reasonably priced. There is an exotic ice-cream dessert menu which is rather tempting.

All Hallows' Church, Mitton

All Hallows' Church at Mitton is a most interesting place. It dates back to the 13th century. The tiled floor slopes down to a wide chancel where can be found a superb screen of oak and cast iron from Sawley Abbey. In days gone by it was customary for the lord of the manor to name himself as rector, but he had to have an ordained priest to take the services. The first known rector was Ralph de Mitton, Lord of the Manor. In 1215 the clergy were forbidden to marry and this led to the church coming under the control of Cockersand Priory.

The present church was built around 1270 and retains its original appearance apart from the chapel which was built by the Shireburnes of Stonyhurst who were descendants of the first Ralph.

It was intended to be the family burial chamber and there is an amazing assembly of recumbent effigies in alabaster. The inscriptions make very interesting reading and an insight to the charitable works of the family to the poor and needy.

The last heir died in 1702, as a child, from eating poisonous berries.

In the chapel is an old, oak chest dated 1637 with three locks, the individual keys were held by the vicar, the lord of the manor and the wardens.

What treasures does it contain I wonder?

Three Fishes Inn
Great Mitton

The Inn has the youngest landlady in this the oldest Inn in Ribblesdale. Its history goes back 500 years when it once belonged to the monks of Whalley Abbey. The three fishes was their official seal, representing the rivers, Ribble, Hodder and Calder. Look for the ancient cartwheel with the word 'ANVNAR' meaning grassland. The cart had only to be used on grassland or else a fine. The preliminary trial of the witches was held here before they were taken to Lancaster.

Whalley Abbey

Whalley Abbey was founded in 1296 by Cistercian monks from Cheshire. The order was founded by St. Robert of Molesme (1027-1111) as a stricter offshoot of the Benedictine Order. The mother house was at Citeaux, France, from whence the Order took its name.
The remains of the Abbey include part of the chapter house and a 14th century gateway. Much of the stone was used in local churches, farms and houses.

Red Pump Inn
Bashall Eaves

There are two red pumps at the Red Pump Inn depicting its origin in 1802 when it was a farm and all the water had to be hand-pumped for domestic and agricultural purposes. This must have been a time-consuming and back-breaking job as cattle require a great deal of water in order to produce milk. There is also a horse-mounting block and tether, again depicting days gone by.

This lone building is situated in this quaint-sounding place of Bashall Eaves. It faces Pendle Hill and offers accommodation with three en-suite rooms. Further investigation of this lovely area is recommended.

There is a dining room offering lunches and evening meals with good food before or after your walk. Mine hosts have won many awards for their cooking which is easily appreciated.

An Inn off the beaten track, but is well worth a visit.

- **Start:** Red Pump Inn, Bashall Eaves. Tel: 01254 826227
- **Distance:** 6 miles
- **Map:** Outdoor Leisure 41. Grid Ref: 695 432
- **Access:** Off the A59 to Clitheroe on the B6243 to Edisford Bridge and Bashall Eaves
- **Terrain:** A flat walk over fields with many refreshment stops in Waddington with much of interest to see.

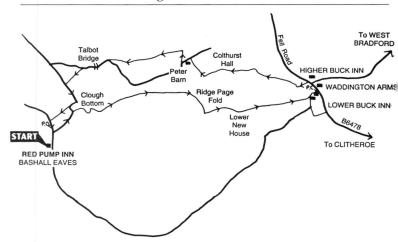

On leaving the Red Pump turn left up the road. After passing the Village Hall, dated 1862, turn right, passing the Old School House. Continue on this quiet country lane to the footpath sign on the right. Follow the hedge on the right, round to a corner and the road at Moor End Farm.

Turn right and left to Clough Bottom Farm (now used as an orienteering centre for business people). Over the bridge, turn right through the farmyard. At the end of the buildings turn left through a gate. Ahead to follow a fence on the right to the second gate (after a new fir plantation). Follow the fence on the left to a gate ahead. Forward to cross a stream to a kissing gate. Follow the fence on the left, crossing two streams to reach Page Fold Farm and a lane.

Turn left over a cattle-grid, to turn right through two gates to an enclosed way (this is an ancient track, here for 900 years, now covered with foxgloves) to enter a field. Turn left to Lower New House Farm, between the buildings. Forward with the wood on the left, over a bridge, to a gate ahead. Follow the hedge on the right, heading for Waddington Church, to reach an enclose lane and The Lower Buck Inn (time for refreshments?).

Continue to St. Helen's Parish Church passing the stocks and pinfold to reach the Waddington Arms.

Head up to the Higher Buck Inn. Up Fell Road. After the toilets turn left into a field to a small gate. Over the stream, turn right to follow it into a field. Forward to a stile, hedge on the right, to a gate, to a stile, turn right to a track. Turn left over Hollins Clough beck to a gate. Ahead, fence on the right, to a stile at the end of the hedge, turn left over the bridge into a field. Colthurst Hall on the right. Bear left to a stile onto a lane.

Turn left to a stile on the right. Bear right to a stile into a wood, over the bridge onto the road.

Turn left passing Peter Barn B&B, to a bridleway on the right. Through two gates to reach a marked post. Turn left, over a stream, up steps to a stile into a field. Straight ahead to cross a farm drive, to the next arrow and bridge. Ahead to the corner of the wood. Follow the wood on the right to cross a stream to a stile. Forward to a stile in the corner. Diagonally right to cross a stream and diagonally right to the road.

Forward over Talbot Bridge to a stile on the left. Follow the wood on the left to cross a stream. Continue to follow the fence on the left to reach a road.

Turn left to a junction. Turn right to the footpath sign ahead at a bend. Follow ahead to reach a road. Turn left past the post office back to the Red Pump.

Peter Barn B&B
Cross Lane,
Waddington
Tel: 01200 428585

The Lower Buck Inn
Waddington

The Inn belongs to Waddington Hospital Trust which was founded by the
Parkers of Browsholme Hall in 1760.

At one time it was also a working farm and a former coaching inn, hence the
mounting block. The Inn still offers accommodation and little seems to have
been changed over the years, resulting in a truly original atmosphere. The
display cupboard in the corner was probably the original low entry into what
was the tap room.

The sign is the Parker's coat-of-arms. The raised foot of the buck represents
the northern sign of the family and the collar the southern side. The white and
red roses of Yorkshire and Lancashire are depicted.

Lunches and evening meals are served seven days a week either in the snug
downstairs room or upstairs in a choice of two dining rooms. Much atmosphere
here.

St. Helen's Church, Waddington

The impressive buttressed tower of 1501, bearing the Tempest arms, overlooks this pleasant, compact village and the handsome almshouses. Much of the church was rebuilt by Paley, 1899-1901, but a 15th-century octagonal font remains, decorated with symbols of the Passion. A recently restored stained-glass panel, depicting Sir Richard Tempest, contains lovely medieval glass. Fine woodwork abounds and innumerable links with local history and families.

The church is dedicated to St. Helen and she is shown in the stained-glass window. On one side of her is Wadda, the Anglo Saxon chief, from whom Waddington takes its name. On the other side is Henry VI who stayed at Waddington Hall, was betrayed and taken back to London to his death. Henry lost the battle at Hexham in 1464.

Next to the church is the pinfold for strayed animals and the stocks for the villagers who went astray and needed punishing. For more serious crimes, local magistrates and assize judges dealt with the culprits.

Waddington Arms
Waddington

The Waddington Arms is just over the bridge in the centre of Waddington. It is a family-owned former coaching inn.

You are sure of a warm welcome for a drink or meal. There is an extensive menu of traditional and continental dishes including vegetarian specials which are freshly prepared each day. The portions are generous and most attractively presented. There is a wide selection of Real Ales in this Free House.

There are four elegant bedrooms and a roof and garden terraces.

Waddington has won many prizes in the best kept village competition. Don't miss the attractive Coronation Gardens.

Henry VI stayed at Waddington Hall for a year before being betrayed to the Yorkists. He escaped via a secret panel and staircase from the dining-room but was captured at Brungerley Bridge.

Copy Nook Hotel
Bolton-by-Bowland

The Copy Nook Hotel is a charming former 17th-century coaching inn of great character with its low oak beams and open log fire.

It is surrounded by open countryside and overlooks Pendle Hill. It is in the picturesque Forest of Bowland National Park. It is possible to stay here in en-suite bedrooms and enjoy the many walks in this area. After a hard day's walking you can return to a guaranteed good meal served in convivial surroundings. Also on offer is caving, fishing, pony trekking and clay pigeon shooting - a wealth of activities or even a very good place to relax.

Lunches and dinners are served including bar snacks with a good selection of beers.

The Copy Nook is a family-run hotel which is famous for its good home-cooked food. English Tourist Board Commended 3 Crowns.

- **Start:** The Copy Nook Hotel, Bolton-by-Bowland. Tel: 01200 447205
- **Distance:** 7 miles
- **Map:** Outdoor Leisure 41. Grid Ref: 776 494
- **Access:** Off the A59 to Sawley, follow the road to Holden
- **Terrain:** A flat walk over fields with much of interest to see in the village of Bolton-by-Bowland.

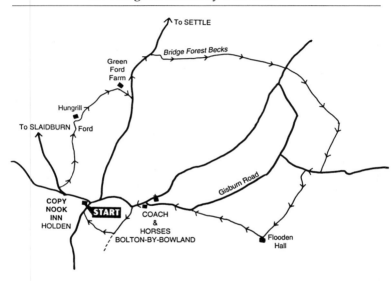

On leaving The Copy Nook turn left and on the road to Holden. At a junction continue on the road to Slaidburn. Turn right, up steps through a very narrow stile. Follow the hedge on the left to quickly cross to the other side of it to reach a stile in the corner. Ahead for approx. ¹/₂ mile to reach a facing wall before Hungrill Farm. Aim for the right-hand corner and gate. Follow the wall on the left to cross a ford to the gate opposite. Follow the wire fence on the right to a gate in the corner. Ahead towards Green Ford Farm. Over the cattle-grid and stream following the signs between the buildings, turn right to a marked small gate. Ahead to the road.

Turn left, on the road to Settle, dropping down and over a bridge.

Turn right at Ivy Cottage, over a wooden bridge. Immediately take the gate on the left, leaving the clear track. Head up into the wood, following the stream on the left to a small gate, leading into an enclosed way. Continue straight forward to reach the road eventually.

Straight across into the yard of Monubent Head Farm to a small gate on the right. Follow the fence on the right, becoming a hedge to a stile in the corner. Turn left into a copse to cross a farm track. Ahead to a trough in the middle of the field. Turn right to a gate on a good track leading to the road.

Turn right to the farm. Turn left passing the new bungalow at the footpath sign. Follow the fence on the right over stile to eventually reach the next stile. Follow the fence on the left to a gate. Turn right on the farm track to Fooden Hall. Turn right to a gate ahead. Bear right to the footpath sign. Follow the fence on the right to a platform stile. Ahead towards the white house. Turn right to the main road.

Turn left passing the School House dated 1874 to reach the Coach and Horses (refreshment time?).

Continue through the village and over the bridge. Here take the footpath sign to Sawley on a good track. At the wall corner ahead, turn right following the arrows and the fence on the right leading through gates to the road.

Turn right back to The Copy Nook.

Fooden Hall

Fooden Hall was once a very fine manor house with its portal entrance and mullioned windows. It was built in the reign of James I (1603-1625). Now it is sadly neglected. Nearby is a mineral spring leaving a deposit of sulphur to cure all ills.

Coach & Horses
Bolton-by-Bowland

The Coach & Horses became an inn in 1801 and faces the village green with its stocks, whipping post and two grinding stones.

This comfortable and hospitable inn offers accommodation and refreshments at lunch times and evenings. There is an intimate dining room with a good selection of dishes.

There are several interesting features including many hunting prints, pewter tankards and an old cash register at the entrance.

Bolton-by-Bowland

Bolton-by-Bowland takes its name from its location - on a bow in the River Ribble. The village is most attractive with two greens lined by attractive properties by Tosside Beck.

Bolton Hall was occupied by the Pudsey family for over 500 years. Unfortunately the Hall is now demolished. At one time it was the home of King Henry VI during the Wars of the Roses. He sheltered here for a year after his defeat at the Battle of Hexham (1464). He discovered a spring in the grounds which is called King Hannah's Well.

Church of St. Peter and St. Paul

The church has some most unusual effigies of Sir Ralph Pudsey who died in 1468. He was married three times and had 25 children. On a slab all his children are carved with their names underneath the carvings of himself and his three wives, Matilda, Margaret and Edwina. His third wife bore him 17 children!

Ralph Pudsey was Lord of Bolton and was knighted by King Henry VI for his faithful support when he was sheltered at Bolton Hall after the Battle of Hexam in 1463. Bolton Hall was unfortunately demolished in 1960, parts dated back to 1334.

The font depicts the eight shields of the families connected with the Pudseys. The oak cover was carved by 'Mousy' Thompson of Kilburn and bears his trademark.

The oak door is dated 1705 and there are 560 studs in it, mostly square pegs in round holes.

Stocks and whipping post

The Parkers Arms bears its name from the Parker family who resided at Browsholme Hall in Bashall Eaves for many centuries. The Inn was built as a hunting lodge and has many stuffed birds and animals adorning the walls. It is classed as an ancient monument which must be preserved.

It occupies a most delightful position overlooking the River Hodder and the impressive Bowland Hills. The exterior is green and white and decorated with hanging baskets. It is a traditional country inn offering a good variety of Real Ales, lunches and evening meals.

There is a most attractive beamed restaurant to seat 55 with glorious views and food to tempt the imagination. There are also four en-suite bedrooms.

Don't miss 'Parkers Ark' which is especially of interest to children with its many animals and birds. The pet and wildlife garden is to the rear. At the front of the Inn is an attractive beer garden.

- **Start:** Parkers Arms, Newton-in-Bowland. Tel: 01200 446236
- **Distance:** 5 miles
- **Map:** Outdoor Leisure 41. Grid Ref: 698 504
- **Access:** Off the A59 to Clitheroe on the B6478 to Waddington and Newton
- **Terrain:** Over fields, country road and with a riverside finish. Much of interest on the way.

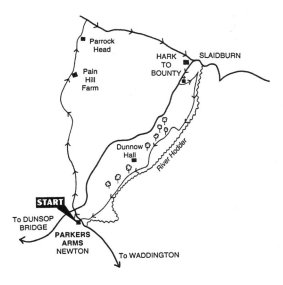

Turn left up the hill to the main road at the telephone box and the footpath sign to Pain Hill Moor. Take the footpath to the right of the house, through the garden, turning right to follow the hedge on the right to a gate and stile ahead. Ahead to the next marked gate. Turn left up to the wall, turn right to the stile in the corner. Follow the wall on the left to a stile. Diagonally left to a hidden stile in the corner. Diagonally right, to a stile in the corner. Turn right to a gate. Follow the wall on the right to reach Pain Hill Farm and the stile in the corner. Bear left towards the white building, crossing a stream up the field to a track to reach Parrock Head Farm. Continue down the drive to the main road.

Turn right passing Ellerbuck Hall (1694) and over the bridge to continue on the quiet road to reach Hark to Bounty Inn. Turn right to the old grammar school and St. Andrew's Church (much of interest here). Round the side of the church to the bottom of the graveyard to enter a field and down to the river.

Turn right to follow the River Hodder turning away from it at a sewage works to reach a clear track. Turn left following the fence on the right. Just before the bridge scramble up the embankment to look at Dunnow Hall. Continue to follow the wood on the right to regain the river. Keep to the fence on the right, to a stile on the right to Newton Bridge. Turn right back to the Parkers Arms.

Dunnow Hall

The Hall has a romantic story to tell. This magnificent house was built in 1860 for Leonard Wilkinson and his bride. He was the nephew of the squire who helped him with the cost of such an imposing residence. Unfortunately his bride died on their honeymoon and the groom was so devastated that he never set foot in the house again. The buillding fell into a state of disrepair.

Recently an Australian couple have made it their home and are painstakingly restoring it to its former glory. The former coach house and stables are to be holiday homes.

St. Andrew's Church, Slaidburn

The amber stone of this old church came from the surrounding fells. The earliest known rector was appointed in 1246 known as Thomas the Parson.

Inside is a unique arrangement of box pews and the 18th-century three-decker pulpit. The Clerk led the congregation's responses from the lowest, the middle one was for the minister and the pulpit which was at the top was used for the sermon.

Another very unusual feature is the two dog whips which were used to control any fighting dogs in church! The Dog Whipper was paid 5/- to 10/- per year for his services.

The Hammerton Chapel was once the site of a fisticuff argument during a service over the seating rights!

Look for the tombstone of the Peel family, relatives of Robert Peel, the founder of the Police.

There are six bells with a wooden frame. These were a gift from the widow of the Rev. Henry Wigglesworth of Slaidburn in 1843. They are seldom rung due to the weakness of the tower which is the oldest part of the church.

There is a Norman font dating from 1229. The cover, which is of oak , is from Elizabethan times.

The inn dates back to the 13th century, and until 1875 was known as 'The Dog', when the squire of the village, who was also the parson, had a pack of hounds. One day, whilst out hunting, he and his party called at the inn for refreshments. Their drinking was disturbed by a loud and prolonged baying from the pack outside. High above the noise could be heard the squire's favourite dog, which prompted him to call out...

'Hark to Bounty'

The inn contains a remarkable courtroom which was in use as a court in 1937. It was visited by the travelling justices from the 14th century onwards, being the only courtroom between York and Lancaster. The records still remain in the Clitheroe Castle Archives and the County Archives at Preston. Set in the heart of the Forest of Bowland, this most attractive stone-built village of Slaidburn makes an ideal centre for those wishing to explore the open moorland, as well as quiet riversides of this delightful and unspoiled area of countryside.

The inn has eight residential bedrooms, all of which have private facilities. The restaurant seats approximately 60 people in cosy, country-style surroundings. In the courtroom up to 120 people can be accommodated. The oak-beamed lounge bar is a very popular meeting place for locals and visitors alike where northern hospitality is paramount, whether it is over a glass of traditional ale or food which tantalises the taste buds.

- ● **Start:**   Hark to Bounty, Slaidburn. Tel: 01200 446246
- ● **Distance:**   7 miles
- ● **Map:**   Outdoor Leisure 41. Grid Ref: 711 523
- ● **Access:**   On the B6478 between Tosside and Newton
- ● **Terrain:**   Over rolling countryside. Much of interest to see on the way.

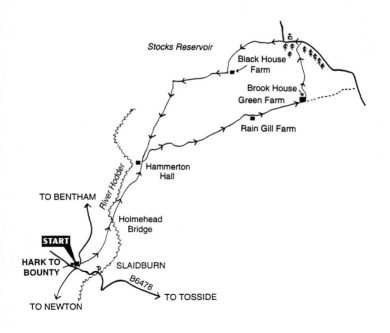

On leaving the Hark to Bounty turn left and left on the road to Bentham. Over the bridge turn right with the River Hodder on the right. Bear left away from the river to a wall corner and a ladder stile ahead by a gate. Follow the wall on the left to reach a clear track. Continue with the wall on the left over Holmehead Bridge. Turn left on the clear track, passing another ancient bridge and up to Hammerton Hall. Turn right and at a junction take the middle gate. Forward a short distance then turning right. Continue to follow the wall on the right and dropping down to a marked gate. Turn left and over the bridge. Turn left, rising up to a marked gatepost. Forward on a green track to a wall corner. Follow the wall on the left, through a marked gate to reach Rain Gill Farm. To the left of the building onto the farm track, continue to follow this to reach Brook House Green Farm.

Here cross Dugdale Syke, turn left to a gate on the right by a footpath sign. Follow the track round with a fence on the right leading to Lower Barn. Throught three gates and ahead to a stile into a wood. Follow the track up to reach a road.

Turn left to reach St. James' Church (pause and rest a while, the door is open). Continue straight ahead on a rough, clear track leading to Black House Farm. Pass in front of the house to the gate on the right. Up to the gate ahead. Follow the wall on the right to a gate and stile leading to an enclosed way (fir wood on the right), to exit into a field. Follow the fence on the right to a gate. Follow the wall on the left to Hammerton Hall on the outward track. Continue to follow the river now repeating the start of the walk in reverse.

At the village turn left to see Slaidburn Bridge and the Riverbank Café for afternoon tea.

Riverbank Café, Slaidburn

Take-aways all day, full meals, snacks, drinks, ice-creams. Bacon butties. Home-made cakes. Tea-rooms upstairs. Very popular with walkers and cyclists.

Riverbank Café, Slaidburn

Slaidburn Bridge

Here was the meeting point for many packhorse routes across the fells. Stainburn is said to be named after a stone slaid or slab marking the spot where many lives were lost in a battle against the marauding Danes. It is the largest village in the area and is most picturesque overlooking the River Hodder. It is a most peaceful setting, but not so in the past due to being border country between Lancashire and Yorkshire which caused much turbulence especially during the War of the Roses in 1455. The first blood was shed at the battle of St. Albans when the Yorkists were victorious. Edward IV was their leader. The war continued throughout his reign with varying success to either side. This caused great hardship to the common people as the rival armies lived by plundering the villages as they passed.

The Moorcock Inn is a most imposing Tudor, timbered building, occupying an isolated position. It stands proud in its beautiful gardens looking to Pendle Hill.

It has a very long and interesting history dating back to 1812 at the time of the Enclosure Act of the common land. Joseph Whittle of Whalley bought 9 acres for £125 and built a small house with a cellar. The Beer House Act of 1830 encouraged the setting up of beer houses to counteract the increased drinking of spirits. This was the start of the Moorcock being used as a public house and resting place for the drovers. For an overnight stay there were grazing pens for their cattle. Not more than three were allowed in one bed and pot luck (a stew of various concoctions), was a few pence!

Today it is somewhat different, having eleven en-suite bedrooms and an excellent choice of cuisine on offer. The hotel is privately run and the family take great pride in offering a warm and friendly atmosphere with its gleaming copper, fresh flowers and oak beams.

What a glorious spot to stay for a longer visit.

Open all year round for morning coffee, lunches, afternoon tea and dinner.

- **Start:** Moorcock Inn. Tel: 01200 422333
- **Distance:** 5½ miles
- **Map:** Outdoor Leisure 41. Grid Ref: 720 465
- **Access:** Off the A59 to Clitheroe and Waddington. On Fell Road on B6478 to Newton
- **Terrain:** An easy, short walk with much of interest to see. A refreshment stop halfway.

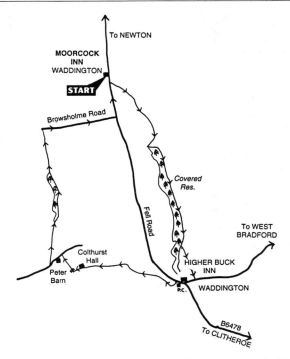

On leaving the Moorcock turn right down the hill to the ladder stile on the left. Diagonally across the field to a gate. Follow the wall on the left on the outside of a wood, cross a ford. To the gate opposite. Follow the fence on the the right, above the beck to a stile in a wall corner to reach Cuttock Clough Farm.

Turn right on the track, over the bridge. Turn left at Tagglesmine Hall to follow the track to a stile by a stream, to cross a bridge. Turn left to continue to follow on the edge of the wood, passing a covered-in reservoir to reach a gate onto a track.

Turn right and almost immediately left, through the undergrowth to a stile in a wall. Follow the wood on the right, crossing a stile to reach a wire fence on the right to a stile leading to a clear track and the main road.

Turn right passing the alms houses (much of interest here) to reach the Higher Buck Inn (refreshment time?).

Turn right up Fell Road and after the toilets turn left into a field to a small gate. Turn right, following the stream into a field. Ahead to a stile. Follow the hedge on the right through a gate to a stile into a wood. Turn right to a track. Turn left, over the bridge to a gate, follow the fence on the right to a stile in the corner. Continue to follow the hedge on the right. At the end turn left over a bridge. Bear left to a gate to reach a lane.

Turn left briefly to a stile on the right. Follow the fence on the right passing Coldhurst Hall to a hidden stile in the corner leading into a wood and a bridge to reach Rabbit Lane.

Turn left passing Peter Barn B&B. Turn right at the gate on the bridleway into a wood. Continue through the wood to a gate and a track at the top.

Turn right to a stile by a gate. Turn left following the wood on the left and later a wall to reach a road.

Turn right on Browsholme Road to reach the main road. Turn left back to the Moorcock Inn.

The Higher Buck
Waddington

The Higher Buck was formerly known as 'The Buck i' th' Vine'. It had a brewhouse, stable and coach house, shippon and warehouse. It has connections with the Ancient Order of Foresters and members were enrolled at the Inn. In 1891 it was licensed by a mother and her two daughters and its name changed to the Higher Buck Inn. Checks were made on the beer quality and doors had to close at 11pm.

Today you will find an open door and good beer to quench your thirst and satisfy your appetite. The Inn is modern and comfortable and a good place to recharge your batteries before tackling the second half of the walk.

The village of Waddington is named after the Saxon leader Wada and has earned the title of 'Best Kept Village' in Lancashire on many occasions. The Coronation Gardens are one of the many attractions.

Almshouses and pump

The alms houses and hospital built in 1700 by Robert Parker, second son of Edward Parker of Browsholme Hall, for the use of poor widows of the nearby parishes.

Edward Parker must have been a philanthropist to endow these cottages and chapel originally for 10 'necessitous widows unable to maintain themselves due to age, ill-health, accident or infirmaty'.

They were required to attend chapel twice a day and received an allowance of £4 per week. Each cottage had a living room and a bedroom with an outside water pump which can be seen today. These homes must have been a veritable haven to the lucky few who were chosen to live there at a time when the conditions of the poor was very hard

During the years more houses were built and repairs and improvements were carried out, new sewers and piped water laid on. The completed improvements were celebrated in September 1893 by a sumptuous repast at the Lower Buck Inn.

The houses are still in occupation by 'needy widows' at the discretion of the Parker Trust.

The chapel is open for a very worthwhile inspection.

The Dog & Partridge
Tosside

The Dog & Partridge is a delightful 16th-century inn, reputed to be the highest in Lancashire. At the time of my visit it was ablaze with flowers.

During the construction of Stocks Reservoir it would have been filled with the 300-400 men who were needed to build it.

The original Norse name for Tosside was 'Tossett'. Tod meant fox and saeter meant hill or summer pasture. Gisburn Forest lies immediately behind the Inn and is managed by Forest Enterprises who endeavour to produce timber and a conservation area. In 1996 £45,000 was spent to provide a recreational site for walkers and cyclists.

At the Inn you will find accommodation at a reasonable price, appetising food and Youngers Ales. An unusual extra bonus is the chance to try reflexology and aromatherapy treatment in the therapy room with Gloria. Just the thing after your walk!

The quiet hamlet of Tosside is half in Lancashire and half in Yorkshire, enabling you to have a foot in both camps!

- **Start:** The Dog & Partridge, Tosside. Tel: 01729 840726
- **Distance:** 8 or 4 miles
- **Map:** Outdoor Leisure 41. Grid Ref: 770 560 (the cycle track is not marked on the map)
- **Access:** On the B6478 between Long Preston (A65) and Slaidburn
- **Terrain:** Easy to follow route, just follow the arrows on the cycle route. Many wildflowers.

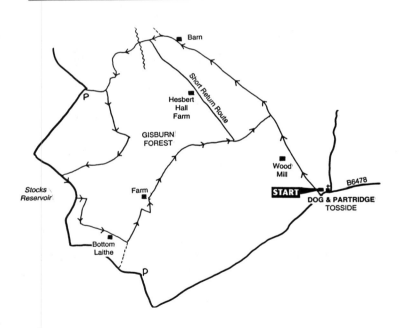

Turn right following the footpath sign up the side of the Inn passing the Woodcutters. At a junction of paths ahead following the arrows on a clear path. After passing a barn on the right, take the next turning left (NOT forward to Martins Laithe). The track goes through the wood, crosses a stream and mounts upwards to come out on the edge of the forest to reach a junction.

For the *shorter walk* turn left and straight ahead back to rejoin the outward track.

For the *longer walk* turn right to cross the river. Turn left at the next two junctions to reach the road between the reservoir.

Turn left on the road and quickly turn left back onto the cycle track, to reach Bottom Laithe. At the junction turn left and before the farm, turn right and right again at the farm. At the next 2 junctions turn right returning to the outward track to return to the Dog & Partridge.

St. Bartholomew's Church, Tosside

A small church built as a chapel-of-ease for the parish of Gisburn. It dates back to 1650 but it was not until 1870 that it became a parish church, serving the widespread rural community. The simple Jacobean pews date to 1694 and the octagonal font was made of stone from the Forest of Bowland. It has a difficult to read inscription regarding the baptism of infants into faith and leading to God 1619.

The old drinking fountain is a memorial to the Queen Victoria's Jubilee in 1887 and also added to Queen Elizabeth 1952-1977.
It is topped by an interesting weathervane, depicting a running fox.

Whitewell is known as 'little Switzerland' because of its location in a deeply wooded valley. There are a few cottages, a church and an Inn at Whitewell.

The Inn is a most impressive former country residence. Six hundred years ago Walter Urswyck, a royal forester made his home here at Whitewell Manor. Red and fallow deer roamed freely on the king's land and punishment for poaching could be death. Walter Urswyck founded the chapel of St. Michael.

A thriving market was held in front of the Inn and the Manor was the 'Swainmote Court' House. The keepers were jury and forest tenants came to Whitewell to give account of their doings.

Look for the initial T and 1836 on the building. This alludes to Townley who is said to have dressed as a tramp and bought the manor for two guineas at a mock auction. When he revealed his identity and wealth the transaction was deemed to be legal.

The present owner is a leasee from the Duke of Lancaster by Grant of the Queen.

Here is a touch of luxury of setting, furnishings and cuisine. Even the loos are something special.

An art gallery, wine merchant and shirt-maker all share the premises and soon I hope my books will be on display!

- **Start:** The Inn at Whitewell, Forest of Bowland, Dunsop Bridge. Tel: 01200 448222
- **Distance:** 7 miles
- **Map:** Outdoor Leisure 41. Grid Ref: 659 468
- **Access:** Off the A59 to Clitheroe on the B6243 to Edisford Bridge to Bashall Eaves and Whitewell
- **Terrain:** Delightful countryside with two properties of distinction to investigate.

Take the road opposite the Inn to the black and white village hall. Turn left, to turn right at the footpath sign up some steps into a field. Bear right to a house and track. Turn round the back of the houses, following a line of trees up to a gate. Bear left to a gate onto the road.

Straight across. Turn right to a ladder stile. Bear left of a plantation to a marked post. Bear right to the next post, bear left to a ladder stile at the entrance to a wood. Through the wood to reach a small gate. Ahead to Crumpton Farm, following the arrows in front of the farm to a clear track to reach the road.

Turn right briefly, to a stile on the left. Turn right through the trees to exit at the top. Follow the fence on the left to reach Spire Farm and the corner of a wood. On an enclosed, narrow way into a field. Head to the left of a brick building diagonally across the field to the corner of a fence and a stile. Turn right to a stile. Ahead to the left of a wood into a field. Ahead to a gate and a clear track. Turn right over a cattle-grid to the road. (Now you are at Browsholme Hall which is well worth a visit.)

Turn left on the main road to turn right over the bridge. Up the bank to a gate. Turn right on a good track leading to Micklehurst Farm. In front of the house to a gate. Forward across the field to a

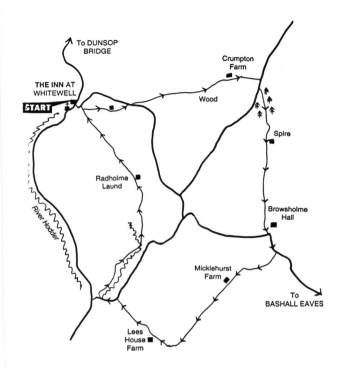

gate and a track to reach a gate by a barn. Follow the fence on the right to a stile. Turn right to a gate, left down to a wood and stream. Turn right to cross a bridge, upwards through the wood to follow the fence on the left to cross a bridge and up to Lees House Farm. Turn right to a gate, ahead to a clear track leading to the road.

Turn left to the sign on the right at the bend. Down to cross a bridge. Turn right to the stile in the fence on the left into a field. Follow the fence round on the right to a stile in a corner. Follow the stream on the right to a farm. Cross the stream, follow the hedge on the left to reach Higher Lees Farm. On the track leading into a field. Ahead to a gate/stile. Ahead to the corner of a wood, following the wood on the right to a stile at a wall/fence corner. Follow the wall up to Radholme Laund Farm. Between the buildings to a gate ahead.

Follow the wall on the right and through two iron kissing gates. Follow the wall on the left to cross the wall ahead and down to a cottage. Across the track to a small gate and the road.

Turn left back to the Inn and the church of St. Michael which is worthy of a visit.

Church of St. Michael

The church dates back to 1521, but it was rebuilt in 1817 largely by the Parker family.

The chapel contains a monument of Edmund Butler (1700-1757) who was the husband of Elizabeth Parker.

There is also a large unusual tapestry on loan from Browsholme Hall. Don't miss the swallow's nest in the porch and the delightful poem about it inside the church. There is also a Bronze Age food preparation mortar found in the riverbed by the son of the house at the Inn.

In the reign of King Henry II, the castle at Clitheroe was built by Robert de Lacy with a chapel dedicated to St. Michael the Archangel, for the benefit of his servants, shepherds and foresters. At the Reformation the chapel was destroyed and the dedication to St. Michael was transferred to Whitewell chapel

Browsholme Hall

Browsholme Hall (pronounced Brusum) is open at weekends during the summer from 2pm-5pm for a conducted tour.

This delightful house is privately owned and has been in the Parker family for 500 years. The name means keeper of the park - the vast land in the Forest of Bowland. They were the bow-bearers appointed by the king to preserve the game.

The original red sandstone house was built by Edmund Parker in 1507. Successive generation have added to the building to make the magnificent house of today.

There is so much of interest to see, one being a cushion cover dated 1450 with the Parker arms and verse. Another rarity hanging on the wall of the entrance hall is a coat worn by Captain Thomas Whittingham from 1665. He was killed at the Battle of Newbury fighting for the king, his wife was Anne Parker.

The panelling, carving, portraits and stained-glass windows are beautiful in this lived-in residence and to tell you more would spoil your discovery of it all.

Open 2pm-5pm, Good Friday & Easter weekend, Spring Bank Holiday weekend, August Bank Holiday weekend, July every Saturday,

There are three pubs in the interesting village of Chipping. The Talbot Hotel was closed for alterations on my visit. Opposite is the tiny, colourful Tillotsons Arms where you will find a most warm and friendly service. It specialises in a wide selection of mouth-watering soups. There is an extensive menu of dishes at reasonable prices which are served at lunchtimes and evenings.

It was originally named The Buck but when it was purchased by Tillotson he gave it his own name.

The name Chipping is derived from the old English word 'Chepyn' meaning market place or barter. The market would have been held in the cobbled square outside the inn, where sheep and woollen products would be brought from the Forest of Bowland.

This picturesque village is on the River Loud. In medieval times there were five watermills on Chipping beck. This is a conservation area of great attraction with a chair factory, cheese-maker and craft centre.

The Sun Inn
Chipping

Higher up the street, opposite the church is The Sun, the oldest inn. Look for the date 1758 and the initials R.H.E. over the door. At that time cock-fighting was held in the backyard and if the weather was bad, inside. Bull and bear baiting also took place. All that remains today is a bull ring in the bar, which is still used as a popular game.

The Inn is haunted by Lizzy Dean, a former barmaid. She was engaged to be married and on the day of her wedding she looked out to the church and saw her fiance coming out married to another. She promptly hung herself in her attic room in the Inn. She died in 1835 aged 20. What a sad tale! What a pity she could not console herself with a pint of good ale and an excellent ploughman's with Lancashire cheese.

Chipping is renowned for its chair-making. John Berry was a founder of this industry. He lost part of his arm in an accident with a circular saw. After this he left his business to his son and became the landlord at The Sun where he was equally successful.

H.J.Berry & Sons Ltd. is now managed by the fifth generation of the Berry family and specialises in rush chairs. The industry started by farmers using their spare time to make furniture, some would become craftsmen. In 1840 John Berry boasted he could make anything from a cradle to a coffin. This started a thriving business manufacturing everything from the log to the finished article.

- **Start:** The Tillotsons Arms, Chipping. Tel: 01995 61568
- **Distance:** $4^1/_2$ miles
- **Map:** Outdoor Leisure 41. Grid Ref: 624 434
- **Access:** Off the A59 on B6245 to Longridge, turn right to Chipping
- **Terrain:** A short pleasant walk over fields and some quiet roadwork. A refreshment stop halfway round.

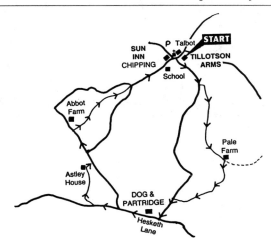

From the Tillotsons Arms walk up the hill and turn left at the Sun Inn on School Lane. Note John Brabin's Old School with its inscription over the door and the new school on the right.

When the houses finish, turn left over the old bridge. Diagonally right to a stile in the corner. Follow the fence on the left, through stiles to reach a stile to the right of Pale Farm with G.T.P. 1788 over the door. Turn right, through a gate, follow the fence on the left to cross a bridge. Head for the house (Dobson Hall). Turn up the access drive to the stile on the left. Ahead to a stile. Turn right, following the hedge on the right to a stile leading to the access drive of Loud Side. Turn left and straight forward following the fence on the right to a stile in the corner. Right to a ladder stile onto a road.

John Brabin's School

Over the door is the inscription - "This schoole founded by John Brabin, Gentleman, Doce Disce Vel Discede 1684" - which roughly translated means Teach, learn, or cut your stick - if you don't want to learn do not enter!

John Brabin was a dyer and a cloth dealer and after his death in 1684 provided funds for a school and uniforms in either violet or liver colour with caps to match! Those who could afford to pay were charged 1d per week for their tuition. He also provided the adjoining almshouses. He was born at a cottage by the post office.

Turn left to reach The Dog & Partridge (time for refreshment?) Continue in the same direction on the road to Inglewhite. After Little Mill Cottage turn right at the footpath sign and next sign by a heap of grit. Follow the beck on the left, turning right to head for a white house (Astley). Cross the fence on the right and make for the footpath sign onto the road.

Turn right to the road junction. Turn left to Inglewhite, up the hill to the footpath sign on the right just before Abbot Barn Farm. Ahead to gateposts. Follow the hedge on the right to a stile. Immediately right over a stile to follow the hedge on the left. Through gate, hedge now on the right to a stile in the corner. Ahead to a gate and cross a stream at the corner. Continue in the same direction to a footpath sign at the road. Follow the road back to Chipping, not forgetting to investigate Saint Bartholomew's Church.

Dog and Partridge
Hesketh Lane

The Dog and Partridge dates back to the 16th century when it was a farmhouse. The attractive and comfortable lounge with its stone fireplace was once the shippon. Here workmen from the nearby lime works could find lodgings; 1d per night in the hay loft and $\frac{1}{2}$d down with the animals.

The Inn was known as The Green Man in the 17th century and later Cliviger Arms. It was the setting of a play written by a local minister and set at "ye Rose room at ye Raven Inn". The Inn was renowned for its rare nutty ale.

Today it is privately owned by the Barr family who take a pride in providing excellent cuisine in a delightful setting.

WALK 19:
The George & Dragon
Wray

The George & Dragon is a typical village pub offering bar food and bed and breakfast accommodation in this interesting setting. In the 17th and 18th century there were two pubs and seven beershops in this busy industrial village. Here was a hive of industry, nail-makers, hatters, cordwainers, weavers, coalminers and quarrymen all needing to quench their thirst. There was no church until 1840 when Wray, a name for nonconformity, became a strong Quaker settlement from the time of George Fox.

The sign George & Dragon refers to England's patron saint who lived in the 3rd or 4th century. The legend concerning his fight with a dragon and rescuing a maiden is unlikely to be true.

JOKE: The rain was pouring down, and it was midnight when a tramp knocked at the door of the George and Dragon, and asked for shelter. "No", snapped the grim landlady, slamming the door. He knocked again, "Still here? I told you, No". "Beg pardon", he said, "But could I have a word with George ?"

- **Start:** The George & Dragon, Wray. Tel: 01524 221403
- **Distance:** 6 miles
- **Map:** Outdoor Leisure 41. Grid Ref: 603 679
- **Access:** Off the A59 to Clitheroe on B6478 to Slaidburn. On the road to Bentham turn left to Wray
- **Terrain:** Great variety and interest, fields, some roadwork, wood and riverside. A refreshment stop halfway round.

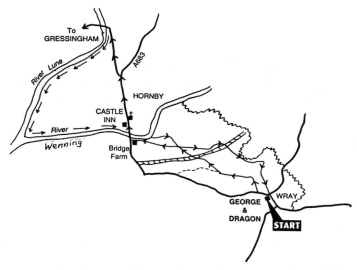

On leaving the George & Dragon turn left onto the main road. Turn right on Lane Head. At a junction of paths, turn left on an enclosed way. Turn through the second gate on the right. Diagonally across the field towards a barn. Take the gate to the right of it leading to a disused railway, to a stile opposite. Diagonally left towards Hornby Castle to a stile in the wire fence. Bear left to a stile at the corner of the wood. Follow the wood on the right round to a stile into the wood, dropping steeply down to the farm, through the yard to the main road.

Turn right over the bridge to the Castle Hotel (refreshment time!).

The Castle Hotel
Hornby

The Castle Hotel is a former 17th century coaching house between the historic city of Lancaster and Kirkby Lonsdale. Morning coffee, lunches, either (bar snacks or in the restaurant), afternoon tea and dinners are available. Also 12 bedrooms, mostly en-suite, all individually styled in-keeping with the traditional 18th century appearance with TV and tea and coffee making facilities. The Inn has a Les Routiers award for good food including game and other local specialities.

You can be assured of a warm welcome whatever your requirements. Here is a good setting for weddings, receptions, private functions for conferences and business meetings.

Hornby has many historical connections. It commands a fine panoramic view of the Lune Valley. Its strategic position has been used for defence purposes over the centuries - hence the castle.

The Loyn Bridge was built in 1684. Here can be found Castle Stede, a good example of a Norman mottle and bailey castle

Walk continued -

Continue up the road passing St. Margaret's Church (worthy of a visit) and Hornby High School. Turn left on the road to Gressingham, passing Castle Stede, an excellent example of a Norman motte and bailey castle. Loyn bridge, built in 1684 over the River Lune, is reached. Take the footpath on the right and turn left under the bridge to follow the River Lune on the right, to join the River Wenning and now heading back for Hornby Bridge and the main road.

Turn right over the bridge and left up the side of the Institute to Bridge Farm. Through the farmyard and round to the left to follow the river on an enclosed track. Bear right at a marked gate and over a stream. Leftwards across two fields. Bear right across two field to a stile in the corner. Follow the wall on the right to reach gates, turn right over the old railway and ahead on an enclosed track to go right through a gate at the end. Ahead through two gates to reach the main road at Wray. Turn left back to the George & Dragon.

St. Margaret's Church, Hornby

St. Margaret's has pre-Norman stones in the entrance, placed there by the founder Colonel W.H. Foster in 1903 which were removed from the old priory at the abbey of Croxton. There are portions of the old cross from the churchyard and the miracle of the loaves and fishes is illustrated. The church has an exceptional two octagonal tower, the upper rotating. The church dates back to 1514. Sir Edward Monteagle built it, though it was not finished in his lifetime.

Hornby Castle

Hornby Castle is privately owned and was built in the last century from the ruins of an older castle built in 1280. It is a most imposing residence of the Foster family.

The castle survived the days of Scots invasion. The Harringtons were here in the 15th century and were implicated in the War of the Roses. The castle was a Royalist garrison and when all other fortresses were taken Royalists figitives, with their families took shelter here. High unscaleable precipices protected it but it was impregnated and overpowered. Cromwell gave orders for it to be demolished.

In the 18th century it was rebuilt by Colonel Charteris. The nearest vantage point is from the bridge. The castle is not open to the public.

The castle has been immortalised in a painting by Turner.

Hornby has many historic connections. Its position commands a panoramic view of the Lune Valley.

Loyn Bridge was built in 1684 replacing a ford. Near it is Castle Stede an example of a Norman motte and bailey castle built as a strategic crossing place of the River Lune.

The Fenwick Arms
Claughton

The Fenwick Arms takes its name from Lady Fenwick who lived at Hornby. She was married to Lord Monteagle. He was the cousin of one of the conspirators in the Gun Powder Plot. He received a letter of warning not to attend Parliament at this fateful time. Lord Monteagle took the letter to the king - James I, who ordered a search of the House and thus was discovered the gunpowder left by Guy Fawkes and his dastardly plot. He was arrested and after torture betrayed his fellow conspirators. They were captured and hanged, drawn and quartered.

The former coaching inn of antiquity is of imposing appearance with spacious, low beamed rooms. There is an extensive menu of reasonably priced food.

The family motto on the coat-of-arms is *Plait us Vivai* which means live to please and I believe this also to be the aim of the Inn.

Lunches and evening meals served seven days a week. Tetley's ale.

The food is attractively served and the portions are generous.

- **Start:** The Fenwick Arms, Claughton. Tel: 01524 221250
- **Distance:** 7½ miles
- **Map:** Outdoor Leisure 41. Grid Ref: 566 667
- **Access:** On A683 between Hornby and Caton
- **Terrain:** An initial climb on very clear paths. A riverside finish. Good views with much of historical interest. A refreshment stop halfway round.

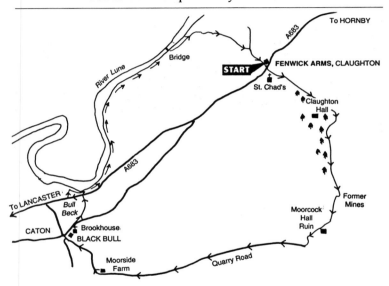

Take the lane opposite the Fenwick Arms with a former mill and a stream on the right. At a junction take the right fork. The entrance to Claughton Hall is reached. Here continue forward, then right round the outside of a wood on a rough track. Continue up with the wall on the left to reach the quarries. Turn right up to Moor Cock Hall, now in ruins, and the windmills to reach Quarry Road. Follow it down to a road junction.

Turn right, passing Moorside Farm and the remains of an ancient cross, to reach a bridge. Turn right to reach The Black Bull, Brookhouse (an alternative start to the walk).

The Black Bull
Brookhouse

The Black Bull is a 16th century inn with a low beamed ceiling which has been extended using the adjoining cottages. In 1823 the Inn was used as a courthouse where the Lord of the Manor ordered his tenants to appear for trial. This was also a staunch Quaker area in the time of George Fox and John Bunyan.

The Inn stands on Brookhouse Bridge which was rebuilt in 1967. Look for the plague stone in it. Note the nearby cottage dated 1683.

The Inn provides lunches and evening meals at reasonable prices. Sunday lunches being a speciality.

Bar Lunches - Evening Meals
Private Parties up to 30 catered for
COME AND MAKE YOURSELF AT HOME
FRIENDLY ATMOSPHERE

St. Paul's Church, Brookhouse

Continue to St. Paul's Church noting its Norman archway. Turn left on Kirkbeck Close to the footpath sign on the right. Between the houses into a field. Bear left to a stile and left to the main road.

Turn left over Bull Beck Bridge. Turn right opposite the lay-by into the wood to a cycle track. Turn right on it to reach and follow the River Lune for nearly 2 miles. When a wooden bridge is reached, turn right, away from the river following the ditch on the left, to cross it to a stile. Diagonally left to a lane. Turn right up to the main road and the Fenwick Arms.

St. Chad's Church is worthy of inspection.

Caton & Brookhouse

Caton and Brookhouse were originally Viking settlements. Caton is known for the fish stones marking the brethren of Cockersands Abbey who sold their surplus salmon to villagers.

A plague stone can be seen built into Brookhouse Bridge. This was a large stone filled with vinegar. Money was put in it before being handled when a purchase was being transacted. Hopefully the vinegar acted as a disinfectant to kill the plague germs. Three thousand died of it in Lancaster alone in 1348-49.

Claughton Hall

This magnificent building is surrounded by woods and agricultural land. The whole estate is fenced to contain the herd of bison. Owen Oyston has owned and farmed the Hall for 25 years. Previously it was sited lower down opposite the church. In 1930 it was moved to its present day elevated position for the view!

The White Lion dates from around 1500 and the outward appearance seems to have altered little over the years. It was a former coaching inn with an adjoining stable. A mezzanine level enabled the passengers to enter their rooms without going outside. In 1829 four customers were caught offering a forged £5 note to the landlady and were sentenced to death. Fortunately for them, all convicted prisoners were reprieved at the close of the Assizes.

In October 1886 the Inn was sold together with Halton Hall opposite, the mill and cottages as part of the estate of Colonel Robert Whittle. A copy of the transaction can be seen on the wall. There are also photos of when the Inn was flooded up to the level of the bar.

The present landlord and landlady both play the keyboard and you may be lucky enough to be entertained by them. Certainly they will provide a warm and friendly atmosphere with home-cooked food at reasonable prices. Lunches and evening meals are provided in this Inn of character and charm.

- **Start:** The White Lion, Church Brow, Halton. Tel: 01524 811210
- **Distance:** 3½ miles
- **Map:** Outdoor Leisure 41. Grid Ref: 499 647
- **Access:** Turn over Caton Lune Bridge, off A683
- **Terrain:** An easy riverside walk to a well known beauty spot - Crook O'Lune. Partly on the Lune Valley Ramble.

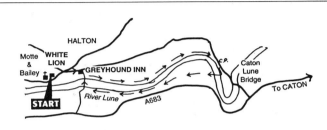

Turn left from The White Lion on the road to Caton to the Greyhound Inn (an alternative start to the walk). Turn down the side of it on Station Road. Turn left on Mill Lane passing Luneside Engineering Company. Continue forward to a stile leading into an enclosed way. At a fork take the left track to cross a bridge into a wood to reach a road.

The Greyhound Inn, Halton

Turn right following the sign to Crook O'Lune car park on an enclosed way. Through the car park and down some steps to a signpost. (If you turn left here you will have a view of the famous bridge immortalised by Wordsworth.) The route turns right following the Lune Valley Ramble leading under a bridge and over an iron bridge into a wood. Turn right down steps to follow the riverside path to enter a wood. Up some steps to a broad track. Turn right on it passing sewage work and a station. Turn right over the bridge to return to the Greyhound Inn and left back to The White Lion. Just beyond is St. Wilfrid's Church and the remains of a motte and bailey castle.

The Crook O'Lune painted by J.M.W. Turner (1775-1851)

Turner was England's greatest landscape artist. The painting is in the Courtauld Institute of Arts, London. In 1816 he did a tour of Lancashire and this illustrated one stage of his journey. In all he did five paintings of this area.

St. Wilfrid's Church, Halton

The church was founded in the 7th century with its ancient cross. Before the Norman conquest the area of Lancaster had been administered from Halton.

97

WALK 22:
The Golden Lion
Moor Lane, Lancaster

Now we have come to our final watering place as did the condemned witches on that fatal day of 20th August 1612. They were taken from Lancaster Castle where they had been imprisoned for four months awaiting trial. They were allowed no defence council or witnesses on their behalf. The damning testimony of a child of nine helped to convict them along with their self-confession, perhaps under torture. Mother Demdike was over 80 years old and died in prison before the trial took place. Nine were found guilty and were allowed a last drink at The Golden Lion, then taken to Gallows Hill, Golgotha where they were hung and the bodies burnt.

We shall never know if they were really wicked people with evil powers or simply the innocent victims blamed for all disasters.

This historic pub has a panelled 'snug' with a local history theme with many photographs and records of the witches. It has been the interest of the landlady over 17 years collecting this vast amount of information.

- ● **Start:** The Golden Lion, Moor Lane, Lancaster. Tel: 01524 842198
- ● **Distance:** 3 miles
- ● **Map:** Lancaster Street Map
- ● **Access:** From A683 on Caton Road, North Road. Moor Lane is off St. John Street
- ● **Terrain:** An easy town walk to see some of the places of historical interest in the city of Lancaster.

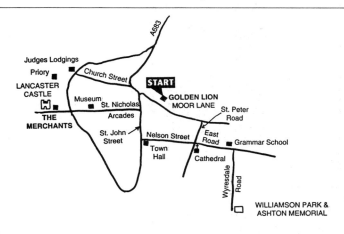

Turn left up the hill from The Golden Lion and over the canal bridge. Turn right on St. Peter's Road to the cathedral. Turn left up East Road passing Lancaster Royal Grammar School. Turn right on Wyresdale Road to Williamson Park. Return back down Wyresdale Road, East Road and Nelson Road to the Town Hall. Turn right along St. John Street. Turn left through St. Nicholas Arcade of shops leading to the Market Square, fountain and the city museum depicting everyday life from the Neolithic age to the present day.

Across China Street to Castle Hill and 'The Merchants' up to Lancaster Castle.

Proceed to Priory Church. Down the hill to the Judges' Lodges and Covell Cross.

Back on Church Street to cross St. John Street back to Moor Lane and The Golden Lion.

Lancaster Castle

This is the Castle Gatehouse and was built around 1400. There is a statue of John O'Gaunt above it. It was his son who built the Gatehouse. John O'Gaunt became Duke of Lancaster in 1362. His son became King Henry IV of England. Both the Castle and the Duchy of Lancaster have belonged to the sovereign ever since.

Today this Gatehouse is the entrance to the prison to confine about 200 people.

To the right of the Gatehouse is the Well Tower where the witches were kept in small, dark dungeons with little ventilation, no sanitation, stone floors and a bed of straw.

The entrance for visitors to the Castle is round to the left. There are regular tours with a guide when you are shown the Barristers' Library and Robing Room. This is where the trial of the witches took place.

Shire Hall was built in 1798 and is used as a civil court. Here can be seen an extensive array of coat-of-arms using a distinctive pattern to identify the owner.

Hadrian's Tower is part of the Norman castle and likely to have been named after the Roman emperor - Hadrian. Here can be seen neck chains, cat-o-nine tail whips and a 'Gossip's Bridle'.

The Drop Room was where the prisoners were prepared for execution. There could be either a long or a short drop. A long drop would ensure a quick death by breaking the neck. A short drop could be up to 15 minutes of strangulation.

Up to 1865 all hangings were in public and watched by thousands of people. 1910 saw the last hanging in Lancaster.

Priory Church

Priory Church was founded by Roger of Poitou in 1094 as a small Benedictine monastery on the site of the present church. This church of St. Mary dates from the 14th and 15th centuries. There are fragments of Anglo-Saxon crosses.

There is a brass recording of the 'talents and excellencies' of Thomas Covell who was keeper of the Castle when the witches were imprisoned here. He died in 1639 aged 78.

Lancaster Town Hall

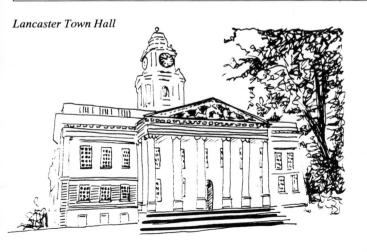

Williamson Park & Ashton Memorial

The imposing dome-topped Ashton Memorial dominates the skyline from its situation at the top of the hill, near where the witches were hung. Williamson Park is set in 38 acres of landscaped gardens with breathtaking views of the sea across Morecambe Bay and the Lakeland fells. It was constructed in 1880 on the site of stone quarries. It was financed by James Williamson better known as the Lino King. He made his fortune in the production of linoleum and oil cloth. Approximately one quarter of Lancaster's population were employed at the mill. His son carried on the business and was conferred with various public offices and honour and became MP for Lancaster from 1886-95. He became Lord Ashton, taking the name from his country estate. During his lifetime he gave £40,000 to good causes in Lancaster including the construction of Williamson Park. The project was carried on by his son James who handed it to Lancaster Corporation in 1881. In 1904 Lord Ashton was responsible for the building of the Ashton Monument which stands 150 feet tall and has a sweeping flight of stairs leading up to it. Three hundred tons of stone were used in its structure.

Today the building houses art exhibitions, information on the life and times of Lord Ashton and a café and gift shop.

Lancaster Royal Grammar School

Lancaster Grammar School came into existence in 1472 when John Gardyner established it with an endowment. After his death the Corporation became responsible for its continuance for the next 70 years. Then befell a disaster, a mill was destroyed by flood from whence came the income for the school's maintenance. The school was closed for 40 years. In the reign of King Charles II the school was rebuilt with two masters. The headmaster received £30 per year and his assistant £15. The master were appointed by the Mayor and the Corporation of Lancaster. In 1824 there were 64 boys at the school. On Shrove Tuesday the boys were allowed to have cock-fights. Another barbaric 'sport' was to throw sticks at a penned cock - the boy who killed it was the winner. The masters claimed the birds for their feast. With this barbaric practice the boys were required to pay the master a 'cock-penny' which was continued until 1824. At this time came the end of free education at the Grammar School.

One of the famous former pupils was Sir Richard Owen renowned for science and surgery. He did post-mortems on the condemned prisoners at Lancaster Castle whence he gained his knowledge of the human body.

Judges' Lodgings & Covell Cross

This was the home of Thomas Covell for 48 years when he was keeper of the Castle.

Evidence at the trial of the witches reported that at Malkin Tower a plot was instigated to blow up Lancaster Castle and kill Covell in order to free those witches who were already imprisoned in the Tower. The plot was discovered in time to prevent a disaster and more arrests were made.

Later the house was used for judges during Lancaster Assizes. It is now used as a Museum of Childhood and Furniture with many examples of Gillows, the famous cabinet maker.

Lancaster is our journey's end here at the capital of this beautiful county. It stands proudly on the banks of the River Lune but there are no ships unloading their cargoes as they did in the past.

Two hundred years ago sugar, rum tobacco and cotton from Barbados and Virginia arrived here. From Ireland came flax for the Lancashire weavers before cotton took its place.

There was a Roman fort in the area of the castle and priory. The Roman camp Anglian settlers named 'Lancaster' from the river 'Lan'.

King George VI created it a city on his coronation day.

Much history has taken place here. Battles a plenty between the Romans, Danes, Normans and Scots, Cavaliers and Roundheads. There is much of interest here to see and discover.